PLANNING FOR BABY'S HEALTH AND HAPPINESS

VINTAGE PREGNANCY AND PARENTING ADVICE FOR MODERN MOMS AND DADS

(AND OTHER CONTRADICTORY ADVICE FROM "EXPERTS")

THE ENTHUSIAST

The Enthusiast publishes books and goods for book lovers. Subjects include, vintage how-to, retro-cooking and home economics, holidays and celebrations, games and puzzles, graphic design, classic children's literature, illustrated literature and poetry, humour.

What's Your Passion?

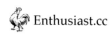 Enthusiast.cc

TheEnthusiast@Enthusiast.cc

ISBN / EAN
1595837566 / 9781595837561

PLANNING FOR BABY'S HEALTH AND HAPPINESS

TABLE OF CONTENTS

ADVICE ON ADVICE

First, Pay No Attention at All

Once your friends and relatives become aware of the fact that you are pregnant, you will be the recipient of all sorts of advice and suggestions from them.

While this advice will be offered with the best of intentions and from the kindliest of motives, pay no attention to it at all.

Preparing for Childbirth: A Manual for Expectant Parents

by Frederick W. Goodrich, Jr., 1966

No Pressure

Sometimes a young mother has so much advice from earnest and well-meaning friends that she is bewildered. Their advice may be good, but sometimes the advice of one friend conflicts with that of another. The baby should not be experimented upon with first one mode of care and then another. Baby care is a great art. It is the most important task any woman ever undertakes, and she should apply to this work with the same diligence, intelligence, and sustained effort that she would give to the most exacting profession.

Infant Care by Martha M. Eliot, 1929

It Gets Easier

The Child who is being raised strictly by the book is usually a first edition.

Unknown

With a Pinch of Salt

The way you treat your children will turn out five years from now to have been completely wrong.

Bill Vaughn

A Humbling Experience

Before I got married I had six theories about bringing up children, now I have six children, and no theories.

Lord Rochester

Opinions, Everybody's Got One

Practically everyone the mother knows—friends, relatives, and neighbors will stand ready to give her advice about how to care for her baby. Much of such information will include the taboos, superstitions, and folklore about babycare.

More-over, friends usually offer advice based on their own experiences, too often forgetting that each baby is an individual with his own particular needs. A wise mother will listen to such advice and then use her own judgment.

Baby Care from Birth to Birthday

by Edmund Griffin Lawler, 1899

PREGNANCY
AND
PREPARING FOR THE BABY

If You Only Remember One Thing

Trust yourself. You know more than you think you do

Dr. Spock's Baby and Child Care, 1945

Don't Quit Your Day Job

It should no longer be necessary for a woman to leave her job or be fired just because she is pregnant.

Prenatal Care,

- U.S. Dept. of Health, Education, and Welfare, 1962

Mother, Can You Spare a Dime?

It sometimes happens, even in the best of families, that a baby is born. This is not necessarily cause for alarm. The important thing is to keep your wits about you and borrow some money.

The Complete Book of Absolutely Perfect Baby and Child Care,

by Elinor Goulding Smith, 1957

BABIES ARE FUN

So you have just discovered that you are going to have a baby. How do you feel about it? Glad or sorry?

I hope you are glad, it is so much fun to have a baby.

Our American Babies; The art of baby care,

by Dorothy V. Whipple, M.D. 1944

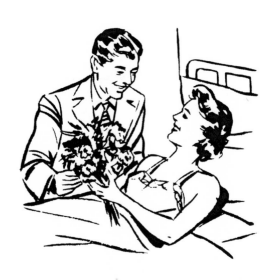

It's All the Same to Baby

If you have time and money, dear mothers, it is very lovely to have all the pretty things you can well afford ; but do not forget to be happy in the promise of your baby, even if the preparation for it must be meagre. It is the baby, not its clothes, which most concerns you, and the world, and its little, blinking self. Wrapped in an Indian blanket, or clothed in purple and fine linen, it is all the same to the baby, if it can but eat and sleep to its heart's content, and its future is not based on the contents, much or little, of its baby hamper.

Maternity Without Suffering

by Mrs. Emma F. Angell Drake, M. D., 1902

It Really Is All About You

In crowded city conditions a spacious apartment is not always possible, but whatever else the rest of the household may have to put up with, the biggest and best chamber should be assigned to the mother.

The Child Welfare Manual

prepared by the Editorial board of the University Society, 1915

You Need Help

During the mother's confinement it is certainly desirable to have someone do the housework. When a second or later baby is born it is essential to have someone to look after the other children.

Our American babies; the art of baby care

by Dorothy V. Whipple, M.D., 1944

And, Take a Bath

If there is any time when a woman has the right to allow herself time to care for her body, money to purchase easy clothes and small personal luxuries, it is when she is carrying a child. Bathing is a luxury which many overworked home-makers deny themselves. The expectant mother should make time to take a daily bath.

Better Babies and Their Care

by Anna Steese Richardson, 1914

The Maternal State

True men and true women hold the very highest esteem for the maternal state, and the opinion of all others matters not; so joyfully go forth to the club, social event, concert, or church; and to do this, you must have a well-designed, artistic dress.

The Mother and Her Child by William S. Sadler, 1916

Well, if I Must

Amusement is, of course, necessary. There is no reason why pleasures should be abandoned, provided they are made entirely secondary to health. So, too, the frequenting of the theatre and of similar places of amusement is often harmless, especially if it is found to exert no unduly exciting influence upon the emotions.

The Care of the Baby: a manual for mothers and nurses

by J. P. Crozer Griffith, 1898

Beauty Surrounds You

Ancient Greeks surrounded the prospective mother with beautiful paintings and statues so as to give a mental impression of beauty to the future generation. They were noted as a beautiful race.

Your Baby A Guide for Young Mothers

by Edith B. Lowry, 1915

Are You Feeliing Febrile Irritation?

The peculiar tendency to febrile irritation, and general plethora, attendant upon pregnancy, the sensibility of the stomach, and its sympathies with the uterus, often causing morbid appetite, nausea, and vomitings, render it indispensable that some attention should be paid to diet.

A Guide for Mothers and Nurses in the Management of
Young Children by Caleb Ticknor, 1839

No Longer an Option...

Doctors differ in their opinions regarding smoking and drinking during pregnancy. Ask your doctor about it.

Prenatal Care

U.S. Dept. of Health, Education, and Welfare, 1962

... And This is one Reason Why

There is of a strong desire to take stimulating drinks during gestation, which, if indulged, is likely to form a habit of intemperance. The annoying sensations created by pregnancy, are, for the time, allayed by stimulants, such as porter, ale, wine, brandy, &c.: but when their stimulant effect has subsided, a repetition of the same remedy is required more than at first.

A Guide for Mothers and Nurses in the Management of Young Children by Caleb Ticknor, 1839

Quit Slopping Around

It is a mistake to take advantage of your "condition" by slopping around the house in old slippers and a messy housecoat, with your hair uncombed. If you can keep yourself neat and well groomed, you may be surprised to find how much the bluest feelings improve.

Prenatal Care, 1962

No Really, You Look Great

For the majority of women, wool is desirable except during the hot weather. A union suit usually is more comfortable than separate garments as it does away with the band around the waist.

Your Baby A Guide for Young Mothers, 1915

Clothes of the Prospective Mother Should Have Quality of Beauty as Well as of Comfort.

You Have Our Permission

During your pregnancy you can be as attractive and comfortable as ever. If you feel and look well, you will continue your social activities with your husband and friends. The time is past when a woman stays at home during pregnancy or goes out only at night. Many women develop a special radiance that offsets the temporary change in their figure.

Parent's Book, c1950

Shameful Shoes

High heeled shoes are an abomination to the prospective mother!

Your Baby A Guide for Young Mothers, 1915

CRAVINGS

Within reason, a pregnant mother should follow her natural appetite and satisfy her dietetic longings. Should she desire unusual articles of food, as far as possible she should have them. The idea has long prevailed that if the mother does not get what her longing soul supremely desires, that the on-coming baby is going to cry and cry until it is given what the mother wanted with all her heart and did not get. Such an idea is the very quintessence of folly and the personification of foolishness and superstition.

The Mother and Her Child, 1916

Have You A Depraved Appetite?

A depraved appetite—that is to say, a desire for unusual, perhaps unwholesome, articles of food—is, when present, a very strong indication of the existence of pregnancy.

Infant Care by Mrs. Max West, 1922

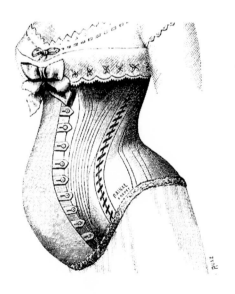

LEARN TO CUT CORNERS

The perfect nursery is built without corners, being rounded in all places where a corner would naturally be.

Mothercraft, 1915

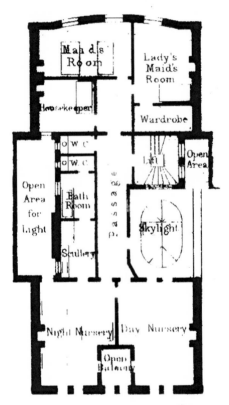

FOURTH FLOOR.

(NURSERIES & SERVANTS' ROOMS)

By M.ʳ Kerr, 1864.

No Mere Dustcatchers

Don't Buy Too Many Things. It's wise to have baby's clothes, bassinet, and furnishings ready at least six weeks before the expected birth date, because babies do sometimes arrive ahead of schedule. On the other hand, the "ahead of time" purchases can be wasteful. Baby "showers" are commonplace for first babies in our society, and relatives will also provide gifts for the newcomer; you don't want to have so many things bought that the gifts will have little use before he grows out of them. Secondly, a lot of things sold to inexperienced mothers as "necessities" for the new baby can be mere dust catchers, seldom used.

Bringing Up Babies; A family doctor's practical approach

to child care. Walter W. Sackett, 1962

A Few Choice Words
For Father

Share Her Enthusiasm

A woman's enthusiasm during the entire nine months should be shared and appreciated by her husband. Probably the fact that it is not is the cause of the silence and misunderstanding in so many homes.

Your Baby A Guide for Young Mothers, 1915

Three's a Crowd (maybe)

Many educators claim that if the marital relations were discontinued during the entire period of pregnancy, the child would profit accordingly. However, this seems to be a question that must, if necessity, be left to the individuals, but in fairness to the woman who is bearing the burden. At this time she should be allowed to decide this question.

Your Baby A Guide for Young Mothers, 1915

THE MODERN MAN

There is no reason why a man cannot do an excellent job of diapering, bathing, formula-making and everything else that must be done for babies. After he gets his feet on the ground, he will probably devise some short cuts that will help his wife.

Living with Baby

by Helen Dudley Bull and Mollie Stevens Smart, 1947

FATHERS, READ THIS TWICE

The Most important thing a father can do for his children is to love their mother.

Theodore Hesburgh

THE OTHER BABY

Do not neglect your husband because you are feeling sorry for yourself. Maybe he is feeling sorry for himself too, because he is worried over what the baby will cost or because you are not so gay as you used to be. He may have his problems too.

Our American Babies; The art of baby care, 1944

LAUNDRY AND LARDER

Just make sure that, from now on, he always has a sufficient supply of clean laundry to see him through your absence. And if he's going to be home alone, stock the larder now with the kinds of foods he's able to manage

Pregnancy Notebook, 1972

THE BIG DAY

AND

ADVICE FOR THE FAMILY

DEPARTMENT OF HEALTH
DIVISION OF VITAL STATISTICS

This is to Certify that a

Certificate of Birth

has been filed for... ....

born on..................... ....whose parents are
(Month)   (Day)   (Year)

.... (Father),

and.. .... (Mother).
(Maiden Name)

....
(Local Registrar)

....
(City, Town, Village)

Free Bowels and Good Hair

When your pains come on, send for your nurse and notify your doctor, that he may be within reach. See that your bowels move freely. Braid your hair in two braids. Have two gallons of boiling water and two gallons boiled and cooled in covered pitchers or pails.

The Care of the Baby, 1917

They Do Grow Up Fast

How fast does a baby grow, in weight, in height, in wisdom and understanding? What should we feed him? How should we clothe him? How can we keep him well?! How can we prevent or cure illness or bad habit? What danger signals should we watch for? These are some of the questions that parents ask, and that this book will try to answer. When a baby is born, whether it is the first one in the family or not, problems come up about his care—how to help him develop normally and how to keep him well. For months the parents have been looking forward to the arrival of the baby and have been making plans. Now that the baby is born the responsibilities of the parents with regard to his care and bringing up become more apparent. They have in their charge an infant who for a long time will be entirely dependent upon them for supplying all his needs. At first only the physical needs are obvious, but the parents must remember that the character building of their child is closely tied up with the way his physical, needs are met. His future mental and physical health will depend largely on the habits he builds during the first year of life, especially in the early months.

Infant Care, 1929

Baby Disappointment, Its a Thing

Many parents are disappointed when they see their baby for the first time. It will take several weeks before your baby loses his wrinkles and red skin and begins to look like the babies you've seen in magazines, or a Parents book.

New York State Department of Health, c1950

The Harsh Truth Is

The truth is that a baby is hoeplessly stupid. He can't read or write or do arithmetic or pay his bills. He is perfectly helpless, and you will simply have to do everything for him.

The Complete Book of Absolutely Perfect Baby and Child Care,

by Elinor Goulding Smith, 1957

A Face Only a Mother Could Love

The new-born baby is certainly not an object of beauty. Even its mother could hardly think it so, did she see it at moment of its birth, before it has experienced the improving influences of its first toilet, wet and more or less covered, as it is, with a peculiar whitish, waxy substance. Still, despite its lack of beauty, its mother loves it.

The Care of the Baby by Griffith, 1895

FIG 19.   BASKET FOR EARLY EXERCISE

Go Easy on Yourself

Q. What is the mistake most mothers of young babies make?

A. They try to do too much. They should stay in bed at least three weeks after the birth of a baby, and should cultivate the habit of resting as much as possible before the birth and during the nursing period. It should be a happy, restful time when sleep, food and exercise are abundant.

What You Ought to Know About Your Baby, 1877

You're Doing Great, Considering

It sometimes is a matter of surprise that young mothers do not make more mistakes, considering their lack of training and experience. In no other line of work do we throw such great responsibilities on the untrained worker.

Your Baby A Guide for Young Mothers, 1915

DIAPER DUTY

If you closely examine the shape of a diaper and the shape of a baby, you will find *no similarity whatsoever.* A person from another planet coming across a diaper for the first time would never in a million years guess its use.

The Complete Book of Absolutely Perfect Baby and Child Care,

by Elinor Goulding Smith, 1957

Don't Forget to Enjoy the Journey

The mother's work is never done, and it seems as there were no time for exercise or pleasure, She cannot find a stopping place where she can leave her work for a few minutes. This is one of the cases where one must "make time" Drop the work if necessary in the midst of the ironing. It Is much better that a family should wear a few unironed clothes than that the mother become worn out, nervous, and cross from overwork.

Your Baby, A Guide for Young Mothers, 1915

How It Should Be

If only more women could be persuaded to let household duties slide for the first two months after baby's arrival the world would be spared many nervous wrecks and many tired, complaining, back-achy, head-achy women. Fewer women would be wrinkled, old and haggard before they are thirty. In the end, keeping quiet for two months, even if it means the employment of extra help, is an economy of time, money and of health.

Baby's Outfit : A book for mothers, 1940

Conflicting Advice on Housework

Housework, with the exception of heavy lifting and scrubbing, is a valuable exercise.

Your Baby A Guide for Young Mothers 1915

Cleaning your house while your kids are still growing is like shoveling the walk before it stops snowing.

Phyllis Diller's Housekeeping Hints, 1966

THE NEWBORN
ALL THINGS BABY
ALL THE TIME

Your Talented Child

There are three things that the newborn baby does very well: eat, sleep, and cry.

Baby Care From Birth to Birthday, 1899

Superstitious Writings on the Wall

Many superstitions have grown up around the mother and the baby. Some of these have had their origin in long past ages; others spring up from time to time. Most of these beliefs are of no value, and many are silly, even dangerous. One of these foolish traditions is that biting (instead of cutting) the baby's finger nails will prevent him from becoming a thief.

Infant care by Mrs. Max West, 1922

Did Someone Say Chocolate?

During the period of night nursing, particularly, a glass of milk, chocolate in some form, or other food may be taken with benefit between the meals

The Baby: A Book for Mothers and Nurses

by Daniel Brown, 1856

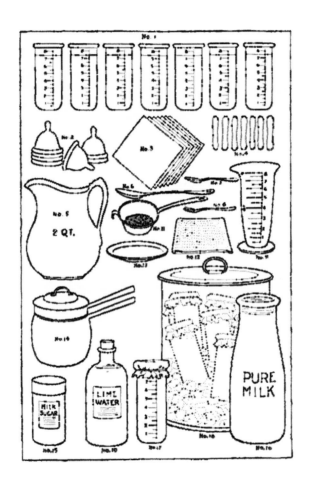

Vigorous Mother

The change which enables more mothers successfully to nurse their infants is due two causes more vigorous fathers and mothers and more vigorous offspring. The making of golf, bicycle and horseback riding, boating, and automobiling popular and fashionable in short, the taking of girls out-of-doors and keeping them there a considerable portion of the day has worked a marvellous change for the better, both physically and mentally. A neurotic mother makes the poorest possible milk-producer.

Short Talks With Young Mothers on the Management of Infants and

Young Children, by Charles Gilmore Kerley, 1909

A Word on Hiccups

Q. What it the cause of Hiccup, and what is its treatment?

A. Hiccup is of such a trifling nature as hardly to require interference.

Advice to Mothers on the Management of Their Offspring, 1839

Brandy Bathing ?!

Q. Is it necessary to wash a new-born infant's head with brandy, to prevent him from taking cold?

A. It is not necessary. The idea that it will prevent cold is erroneous, as the rapid evaporation of heat, which the brandy causes, is more likely to give cold than otherwise.

Advice to Mothers on the Management of Their Offspring, 1839

No Baby Kissing...

We most strongly protest against the haphazard, promiscuous kissing of babies.

The Mother and her Child, 1916

... Well, If You Must ...

If baby is the first one that has graced the household, and must be kissed, this can be accomplished with the least damage if the kiss is implanted on the head or forehead.

Short Talks with Young Mothers, 1863

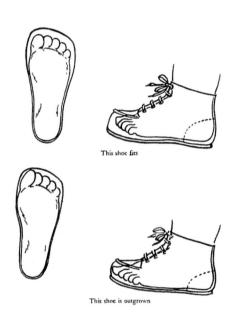

This shoe fits

This shoe is outgrown

If the Shoe Fits

As soon as an infant tries to stand and before he learns to walk he should begin to wear shoes fastening around the ankle. The shoes should have soles that are firm, flat, and moderately flexible, of medium weight, made of rough leather or elk hide, so as not to be shiny nor slippery. Such a sole allows the baby's foot to take its natural position.

Infant Care, 1929

DUELING GRANDMOTHERS

One grandmother will spoil a baby. Two working together will bring him up in the way he should go, for each will suspect the other of spoiling him and will check it.

William Allen White

INFANT TOSSING

Q. Do you approve of tossing an infant much about?

A. Violent tossing of a young infant should never Be allowed; it openly frightens her. She should be gently moved up and down (not tossed!)

Advice to Mothers on the Management of Their Offspring,

1839

Are They All Working Against You?

The cooperation of the father, too, must be secured or all the efforts of training are futile. Very often the mother finds that with her the child's behavior is perfect, but as soon as the father comes home all the bad habits are repeated. The worst sinners of all, however, are usually the grandparents, especially the grandmother, and her influence is particularly pernicious, as she is supposed by her previous experience to know everything about babies.

The Happy Baby by Emmett Holt, 1924

FEW AND GOOD

Don't let your child have many toys. "Few and good", is the slogan. Do you know a sadder figure than the blase young victim of the overloaded Christmas tree?

Sets of toys which may be bought one-at-a-time develop the collecting instinct and keep alive the appetite. The circus may be gathered, animal by animal, and clown by clown; the farmer set in the same way, farmer, wife, cow, barn — to completeness.

Mothercraft, 1915

Is Gin Good for Babies?

Q. If a child be suffering severely from wind, is there any objection to the addition of a small quantity of gin to his food to disperse it?

A. It is a murderous practice to add gin to the food!

Advice to Mothers on the Management of Their Offspring, 1839

And It Is a Real Art

The art of being a parent is to sleep when the baby isn't looking.

Unknown

Don't Be a Food Sneak

Another thing is the practice of sneaking the food in while the baby's mouth is hanging open with wonder at some new diversion or story. It is truly amazing into what trouble this can lead you, because he will be constantly demanding bigger and better stories.

To sum up this brief discussion I will simply say this. If your child won't eat, first be sure he is well. Then keep cool; don't let him get you excited; be nonchalant—even if you don't light a cigarette.

Let's Talk About Your Baby, 1947

First Season Review

Usually we do not consider that a baby of one year of age has a great deal of knowledge, but, when we compare its knowledge with that which it had at birth, we find it has made considerable advancement during the year.

Your Baby A Guide for Young Mothers, 1915

Reasonable Q. Ridiculous A.

Q. Should any attempt be made to develop a young baby's mind?

A. No. A baby should not even be played with, or in any way excited. This makes it nervous and gives it indigestion.

What you Ought to Know about your Baby , 1877

Wholesome Neglect

Nowadays, among the prosperous classes, we often find over-care of babies instead of under-care. The one is as unprofessional as the other. Dr. Charles G. Kerley, a pediatrician whose patients are among the wealthy of New York, tells mothers that he wishes every baby were twins, so that there would be some wholesome neglect of one, at least, while the other was being coddled.

Mothercraft, 1915

In Defense of Mud Pies

A kind word ought to be spoken of the good old sport of making mud pies. Let us appeal for a little indoor play with mud. When the day is rainy and long, a little well washed mud may be brought in and put on the Kitchen table or floor to give delightful sport to the well-aproned youngster.

The Child Welfare Manual, 1915

Suck It Sigmund

And again, when I see the opinion expressed that thumb-sucking in infancy is an indication of an abnormal sex tendency, I am inclined to agree with Dr. John L. Morse, who says that the abnormality is more likely to be present in the author of such a statement than in the child. So, just let me warn you to do all your reading of psychology with a wide-open and critical mind, and if what you read, especially about sex, does not appeal to your common sense, then discard it.

Let's Talk About Your Baby, 1947

Discipline, Character Building, and Other General Parenting Advice

And Yet We Must

Setting a good example for your children takes all the fun out of middle age

Unknown

HYPNOPÆDIA ANYONE?

It is claimed that wonderful results have been obtained by having the mother talk to her child while it is sleeping in a quiet well-modulated voice, the thing she wished to impress upon the child. For instance, the mother sitting by the bedside of the baby that has been irritable and cross might say, "Tomorrow baby is going to be good. He is going to have a nice sleep now and when he awakens he will feel so rested and will be such a good boy."

Just how much can be accomplished by this procedure is a matter for conjecture, but at any rate a trial can do no harm.

Your Baby A Guide for Young Mothers, 1915

Mold Their Little Minds

A little child is so easily influenced that we can mold it into almost any form we choose and work for. Is it not within the reach of all parents to-day, with our public schools and colleges in almost every town, with books so cheap that they seem within the reach of all, with advantages that were wanting years ago now at our hands; does it not seem possible for all parents to give their children a start and onward push in almost any direction ? ... Look up, and your children will follow your eyes; look down, and they will do the same.

Maternity Without Suffering, 1902

TRUTHFULNESS

Example is more valuable than precept in the instruction of children, for they are wonderful imitators both in word and action; hence, a child should never be told a falsehood by a parent or nurse for the sake of gaining the child's obedience.

Our baby; a concise and practical guide for the use of mothers in the care and feeding of infants and young children, 1912

SOCIALIST OFFSPRING

If we teach our offspring to expect everything to be provided upon demand, we must admit the possibility of sowing the seeds of socialism.

Bringing up Babies: A Family Doctor's Practical Approach to Child Care, 1962

TRUTH

Makeshift, contemptuous, humorous, or cynical answers should never be given to a child, however young. A parent should do his or her level best to give a simple and satisfactory answer to the child's questions. This is at times extremely difficult. Indeed, one answer may suggest a dozen other insistent " whys." Yet a parent should realize that it is a crime to tell an un-truth to a child, through, for instance, some mistaken notion of prudery, and that however great the effort to give a fair and simple answer to a question, it is well worth the trouble to set a child on its course without furnishing it with a mass of mental furniture of which it must un-burden itself sooner or later.

The Baby : A mother's book by a mother

You're Going to Wear That?

There is no justification for controlling a child's tastes. If it wishes to wear crimson satin (and it is procurable), in which it would look hideous or startling, it is very unwise to forbid it. The child should be told that it is an unsuitable dress ; and when this has been enlarged upon, if the child persists, it should be allowed to make itself hideous. It will soon learn if the taste of those about it, and the pictures and decorations of the home, are beyond cavil. I do not think there can be much worse influence on a child's mental and moral development than the conviction that it is hampered by arbitrary commands and prohibitions.

Baby's outfit : A book for mothers, 1940

ADVICE ON SITTERS

As I envision the perfect sitter, she should do just that: sit. For the normal evening out she should have little to do but watch for evidences of fire, flood, or other emergency, because Baby is almost invariably tucked away in bed for the night by the time Mother and Dad leave home. If the sitter is a reliable person who won't drink any alcoholic beverages on the job (or call in her crowd for a jam session, if she be a teenager) her duties should be simple indeed. Just let her know what to do if Baby cries (and be specific about what not to do,) how she can reach you by telephone, and give her any other instructions that may be appropriate.

Bringing up babies; a family doctor's practical approach to child,

1962

Happy Home

There is one thing every baby needs whether he is born in a palace or in a cabin. Of all the things you will provide for your baby this one is by far the most important of all. All the money in the world cannot buy it. It is sometimes found at its very best in the humblest of homes, sometimes too, it is found in the lap of luxury. But wherever it is found, the baby who grows up with it is pretty apt to have a good start in life. This thing is a happy home, a home where kindliness, consideration and genuine affection among the grownups make the atmosphere that warms the heart of all who enter into its charmed circle.

Our American Babies; the art of baby care, 1944

Put The "Fun" In Fundamentals

One day I asked Dr. Ira S. Wile, to formulate a very brief creed stating the fundamentals of a child's right living.

Here are the articles of the creed:

- Plenty of air, which includes sunshine.
- Plenty of rest.
- Plenty of water. (This means both within and without.)
- Moderate and nourishing food.
- Moderate clothing — ask yourself if the child is coolly enough dressed rather than warmly enough.
- Plenty of play.
- Plenty of common-sense.
- Which last, being interpreted, means the wisdom and the initiative to adapt all laws to your individual conditions.

Mothercraft, 1915

In All Things, Balance

Many untrained individuals have wrong ideas concerning what constitutes proper care of children. They are liable to go to one of two extremes. Either they are over-indulgent or they are too severe. The one disregards all rules of hygiene and refuses to conform to any regulations "because the baby does not want it," The undeveloped child is allowed to eat and sleep when it pleases, to follow its own caprice in all matters without regard to the effect upon its health or without consideration for the remainder of the family. The other extremist is over-anxious concerning every detail of the child's life. The over-watched child is not allowed to drink one drop more than the rules prescribe. A variation of a few minutes in its hours of sleeping is watched with concern. The baby is wrapped and toasted and kept so like a hothouse flower that it does not develop any power of resistance. One of these extremes is as had as the other.

A great deal of judgment and common sense, with a foundation of knowledge, is necessary for the proper care of babies.

Your Baby A Guide for Young Mothers 1915

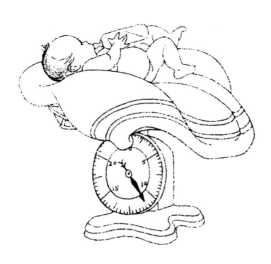

YOU STEER

In automobile terms, the child supplies the power but the parents have to do the steering.

Dr. Spock's Baby and Child Care, 1945

BABY NAMES

What's in a Name?

In choosing a name for your baby, be sure to consider the following:

1. Does it roll off your tongue smoothly when said with your last name?
2. Is it one which your children will be certain to like throughout the years?
3. Be sure that the name and initials together with the last name will not lend itself to an unpleasant nickname.
4. If the name can be shortened at all, be sure that it is pert.

Baby's Own Story, 1950

Baby Names Advice

There is much to be considered in naming Baby and making a wise choice is not always easy. Baby's name is one of the intimate things he is to cherish. It touches the spirit of him and goes with him inseparably through life. A child can live up to a worthy name. Give him a good one and he has just that much more chance of being good. The choice should not be left to chance or to trivial circumstances. It should not be determined solely by tradition or by mistaken notions of family obligations. There may be any number of fond relatives who hope or expect to be honored by a namesake but it is hardly fair to a child to burden him with a long string of names to appease family feelings. Choose for him a good, strong name. Sturdy names that savor of the life of plain folk are found, when their origin is traced, to derive from true aristocracy. They "wear better" than elaborate sounding names that may be in vogue today and not in such good taste when Baby grows to manhood or womanhood. Take John, for instance. Since the days of Christ this name, John, the beloved, has lived. How much better it is than Marmaduke, Montmorency or some other fancy name. It is well to put your choice of a name to the following test:

- Does it sound well with the last name?
- Has it favorable significance?
- Is it appropriate to the probable appearance or temperament of the child?
- For instance, brunette children are misnamed Blanche or Lily.
- Is the name manly, if Baby is a boy?
- If Baby is a girl, will the name "wear well"? It should not be so elaborate as to appear affected.

The Baby : A mother's book by a mother

BOY'S NAMES

NAME	MEANING	ORIGIN
Abel	Breath	Hebrew
Abraham	Father of a multitude	Hebrew
Adam	Of the earth	Hebrew
Adolph	Noble hunter	German
Adrian, Arne	Dark complexion	Latin
Albert	All bright	English
Albin	Light complexion	Latin
Alexander	Helper of men	Greek
Alfred	Counselor	Teutonic
Algernon	Venerable	French
Allan	Cheerful	Keltic
Amos	Burden bearer	Hebrew
Anatole	Eastern Man	Greek
Andrew, Andree	Manly	Latin
Angelo	Celestial	Italian
Anthony	Flourishing	Roman
Archibald	Holy prince	Teutonic
Armand, Armin	Public man	Teutonic
Arnold	Eagle power	Teutonic
Aron	Strength	Hebrew
Arthur	Powerful	Keltic
Arvid	Eagle of the woods	Scand.
Augustus	Illustrious	Latin
Axel	Divine reward	Danish
Barry	Honorable	Keltic
Bartholomy	Son of furrows	Hebrew
Basil	Kingly	Greek
Benjamin	Favored son	Hebrew
Bertram, Bernard	Mighty hunter	Teutonic
Birger	Warrior	Teutonic
Boyd	Fair, light	Keltic
Brian	Strong speaker	Keltic
Bruce	Immortal	Greek
Bruno	Brown	Teutonic
Byron	Strength	Keltic
Calvin	Courageous	Latin
Cecil	Harmonious	Latin
Chester	Sound man	Teutonic
Charles, Carl	Man, courageous	Teutonic
Chauncey	Estimable	Saxon

Name	Meaning	Origin
Christian	Believer in Christ	Greek
Clarence	Bright	Latin
Claude	Gentle	Roman
Clement	Merciful	Latin
Clifton, Clive	Cliff dweller	English
Clinton	High born	Teutonic
Colin	Man of the people	Saxon
Conan	Wisdom	Keltic
Conrad	Able speaker	Teutonic
Cornelius	Enduring	Latin
Craig	Steadfast	Teutonic
Curtis	Courteous	English
Cyril	Lordly	Greek
Daniel	Judge of God	Hebrew
David	Beloved	Hebrew
Dennis	Of Dionysos	Greek
Dermot	Freeman	Keltic
Desmond	Destined to rule	Latin
Dion	People's ruler	Teutonic
Donald	Proud chief	Keltic
Douglas	Dark complexion	Keltic
Duke	Noble chief	Teutonic
Duncan	A born chief	Keltic
Earl	Chief	Teutonic
Eberhard	Big game hunter	Teutonic
Edgar, Edmund	Warrior	Teutonic
Edward	Rich guardsman	Teutonic
Edwin	Rich friend	Teutonic
Ellis, Elliot	God is the Lord	Hebrew
Emil	He who works	Latin
Emery	Work master	Teutonic
Enoch	Dedicated	Hebrew
Erick	Ever king	Teutonic
Ernest	Sincere	Teutonic
Ethan	Wisdom	French
Eugene	Noble birth	Latin
Evan, Everett	Young warrior	Teutonic
Fabian	Bean grower	Latin
Felix	Happy lad	Latin
Ferdinand	Adventurer	Teutonic
Francis, Frank	Free, Liberal	Teutonic
Frederick, Fritz	Peace Ruler	Teutonic

Name	Meaning	Origin
Gabriel	Faithful worshiper	Hebrew
Gail	Valour	Keltic
Gaston	From Gascon	French
Gebhard	Strong giver	Teutonic
Geoffrey	Peaceful	Teutonic
George	Husbandsman	Greek
Gerald	Fair of face	Gallic
Gerar'd	Soldier	Teutonic
Gilbert	Fair pledge	Teutonic
Glen	Sunny	American
Godwin	Friendly	Teutonic
Gordon	Generous	Gallic
Gregor	Watchful	Greek
Gustav	Goth's staff	Norse
Guthrie, Guy	Good sense	Keltic
Harold	Powerful	Norse
Harry, Henry	Home ruler	Teutonic
Hector	Defender	Greek
Helge	Holy man	Teutonic
Helmar, Herbert	Warrior	Teutonic
Hiram	Jolly	English
Homer	Sociable	Greek
Honore	Honored	Latin
Horace	Prudent	Latin
Howard	Honorable	Keltic
Hubert, Hugo	Bright mind	Teutonic
Humphrey	Peaceful	Teutonic
Irvin, Ira	Calm	Greek
Isaac	Merry	Hebrew
Isadore	Gifted	Greek
Isham	Swordsman	Teutonic
Ivan	Bow bearer	Teutonic
James, Jacob	Supplanter	Hebrew
Jerome	Holy name	Greek
Jerry	Exalted of God	Hebrew
John, Jean	Gracious	Hebrew
Joseph	His people will increase	Hebrew
Justin	Just	Latin
Julius, Julian	Conqueror	Latin
Kay	Rejoicing	Latin
Kenneth	Comely	Keltic
Klaus	Victorious	Teutonic

Name	Meaning	Origin
Lambert	Good natured	Teutonic
Lawrence, Larry	Of laurel, gay	Latin
Leander	Lion tamer	Greek
Lear	Of the sea	Keltic
Lee	Gentle	Keltic
Leif	Relic	Norse
Leigh	Of the country	Keltic
Leo, Leonard, Lionel		
	Lion like	Greek
Leroy	Royal	French
Lester, Leslie	Lustrous	Saxon
Levy	Bond of union	Hebrew
Lewis, Louis	Famous warrior	Teutonic
Llewellyn	Lightening	Keltic
Lloyd	Venerable	Keltic
Lovell	Lovable	English
Lucas, Lucian	Bright light	Latin
Luther	Famous warrior	Teutonic
Lyle	God fearing	Hebrew
Magnus	Great man	Latin
Malcolm	Servant of Columbia	Keltic
Marshall	Martial	Latin
Martin, Morton	Military	Latin
Matthew	Gift of God	Hebrew
Maurice, Morris	Of the Moors	Latin
Melvin	Happy chief	Keltic
Meredith	Sea protector	Keltic
Merwyn	High of the sea	Keltic
Michael	Glorifying God	Hebrew
Miles, Milton	A soldier	Greek
Morgan	Seaside dweller	Keltic
Moses	Foundling	Hebrew
Murdoch	Marine man	Keltic
Napoleon	Of the new city	Greek
Nathanael, Nathan		
	Gift of God	Hebrew
Neal	Chief	Keltic
Nestor	Superior	Greek
Nicholaus, Niels	Victory of the people	Greek
Noah	Restful nature	Hebrew
Noel	Born on Christmas day	Latin

Name	Meaning	Origin
Norman	Man from the North	Teutonic
Octave	Eight	Latin
Olof, Ole	Ancestors relic	Scand.
Oliver	Peaceful	Latin
Orlando, Orville	Fame of the land	Teutonic
Oscar	Soldier of fortune	Keltic
Othello, Otto	Rich man	Teutonic
Owen	Young warrior	Keltic
Patrick	Noble man	Latin
Paul	Small of stature	Latin
Percival, Percy, Perry		
	Courteous	Latin
Peter, Pierre, Pehr		
	Firm	Greek
Philip	Lover of horses	Greek
Quentin	The fifth	Latin
Raynor	Warrior	Teutonic
Ralph	Counselor	Teutonic
Ramon	Dark prince	Teutonic
Raoul, Rolph	Highly famed	Teutonic
Raphael	Heading God	Hebrew
Raymond, Ray	Wise protector	Teutonic
Reginald	Powerful	Teutonic
Reuben	Behold a Son	Hebrew
Richard, Ritchie	Stern King	Teutonic
Robert, Rupert	Bright fame	Teutonic
Roger, Roland	Swordsman	Teutonic
Rory, Roy	Red	Keltic
Russell	Brown	Latin
Rudolph	Famed hunter	Teutonic
Samuel	Asked of God	Hebrew
Saul	Longed for	Hebrew
Seth	Appointed	Hebrew
Silvester	Living in the woods	Latin
Simon	Obedient	Hebrew
Solomon	Peaceful	Hebrew
Spencer	Hope	Latin
Stacy	Resurrected	Greek
Stanley	Camp glory	Slav
Steen, Sten	Stone	Teutonic
Stephen	Crowned	Greek
Sune	Jolly, sunny	Scand.

NAME	MEANING	ORIGIN
Sven	Youth	Scand.
Terence, Terry	Kind	Latin
Theodore	Divine gift	Greek
Thomas	Twin	Aramic
Thor, Tore	The God of thunder	Norse
Timothy	God fearing	Latin
Tracy	Produce merchant	Greek
Tristan	Hero	Keltic
Ulric	Noble ruler	Teutonic
Ulysses	Haughty	Latin
Valentine	Good health	Latin
Victor	Conqueror	Latin
Viking	Bay inhabitant	Scand.
Vincent	Conquering	Latin
Virgil	Flourishing	Latin
Walter, Wallace	Powerful fame	Teutonic
Warner, Warren	Protector	Teutonic
Wayne	Adventurer	Teutonic
William, Willis	Resolute ruler	Teutonic
Wilmar, Wilbert	Famous	Teutonic
Zacharias	The Lord will remember	Hebrew

This Might Just Work

The Fact is whatever name you choose, the baby, some years hence, will hate it anyway... If the baby is a girl however, you can give her a middle name and as soon as she's old enough to talk, tell her that the middle name is her first name. Then when she's fourteen... she'll decide to use her middle name for a first name and everything will come out right after all.

The Complete Book of Absolutely Perfect Baby and Child Care,

by Elinor Goulding Smith, 1957

NAME	MEANING	ORIGIN
Abby	Sweet refuge	Hebrew
Ada	Pretty maiden	Hebrew
Agnes, Inez, Agda		
	Moral, pure	Latin
Alberta, Albrette	All bright	English
Alexandra	Altruist	Greek
Alfreda	Counselor	Teutonic
Alice, Adele, Adelina		
	Nobility	Teutonic
Alma	All good	Latin
Alwina	Much beloved	Teutonic
Amanda	Lovely	Latin
Amelia	Flatterer	Greek
Amy, Amelita	Beloved	Latin
Andree, Andriette	Strength	French
Angela	Angelic	Italian
Anna, Anita, Nancy		
	Graceful	Hebrew
Astrid	True love	Norse
Audrey	Mild, noble	English
Augusta	Venerable	Latin
Aurelia	Golden	Roman
Aurora	Dawn of day	Roman
Antoinette	Flourishing	Roman
Aveline	Pleasant	Norse
Barbara	Stranger	Greek
Beatrice	Luck bringer	Latin
Bernice	Victorious	Greek
Bertha, Belinda	Bright	German
Beryl	Spiritual	English
Beulah	Married bliss	Latin
Blanche	White	Latin
Bonnie	Good	French
Bridget, Britta	Strength	Keltish
Brunhild	Blond maiden	Norse
Camille	Messenger	Latin
Candide	White spirit	French
Cara	Friend	Keltic
Carmen	Beloved	Spanish
Caroline, Carol	Bold	Latin

99

Name	Meaning	Origin
Catherine, Cathryn	Pure, innocent	Latin
Cecilia	Lover of harmony	Latin
Celeste	Lofty manner	Roman
Charlotte	Bold	Latin
Charmaine	Charming	French
Christine	Christian	Latin
Clara, Claire	Bright	Latin
Conchita	Deeply religious	Spanish
Colleen	Darling	Irish
Constance	Steadfast	Latin
Consuelo	Consolation	Spanish
Corinne	Maiden	Greek
Cordula	Jewel of the sea	Keltic
Cornelia	Enduring	Latin
Cynthia	Delightful	Greek
Cyrilla	Lordly	Greek
Dagmar	Celebrity	Danish
Daisy	Flower	English
Darby	Freeborn	Irish
Delia	Brave	Greek
Desiree	Lovable	French
Diana	Blond goddess	Latin
Dolores, Lolita	Sorrow	Latin
Dorothy, Doris	Gift of God	Latin
Drucille	Noble	Roman
Duane	Protector	French
Ebba	Courageous	Scand.
Edith, Enid	Wealth	Anglo-Sax.
Edna	Happiness	English
Eleanor, Lenore	Radiant, light	Greek
Elfrida	Fairy child	Teutonic
Elizabeth, Lizzie	God's worshipper	Hebrew
Ella, Ellen, Eileen	Shining light	Anglo-Sax.
Elsa, Elsie	Noble, cheerful	Teutonic
Elvera, Elva	High birth	Spanish
Emerald	Gem	Ancient
Emilia, Emily	Flatterer	Greek
Emma	Great	German
Erminia	Noble lady	Latin
Ernestine	Serious	Teutonic

100

NAME	MEANING	ORIGIN
Esther, Stella	Star	Persian
Ethel	Noble speaker	English
Ettora	Defender	Italian
Eugenia	Well born	Greek
Eunice	Victorious	Greek
Eulalie	Able speaker	Greek
Eva, Evelyn	Life	Hebrew
Evangeline	Lord's messenger	Greek
Ernie	Happy	Scotch
Faith	Faithful	English
Fanchon	Freeborn	French
Felicia	Ever good	Latin
Fernanda	Bold	Gothic
Flavia	Blond, fair	Latin
Florence, Flora	Flower, lovely	Italian
Frances, Fanny	Freeborn	Teutonic
Frederica, Frieda	Princess of peace	Teutonic
Freya	Goddess	Scand.
Fylgia	Sea maid	Swedish
Fay	A fairy	French
Gabrielle	God's heroine	French
Gay	Happy maiden	English
Genevieve	Peaceful	French
Geraldine	The fair	Gallic
Germaine	Father's child	French
Gertrude, Gerda	True	Danish
Georgia	Farmer's wife	Greek
Gladys	Lame	Latin
Glee	Cheerful	American
Gloria	Glory	Latin
Godiva	Divine gift	Teutonic
Goldie	Golden hair	American
Grace	Good will	Greek
Gurley	Maiden	Swedish
Gwendolyn, Gwen		
	Fair	Welsh
Hazel	Brown eyes	English
Hedvig	War refuge	Danish
Henrietta	Home ruler	Teutonic
Hilda, Hildur, Hildred		
	War maiden	Norse
Hope	Hopeful	American

NAME	MEANING	ORIGIN
Hortense	Girl of the garden	Greek
Hulda	Kind	Scand.
Ida, Ina	Rich gift	German
Idun	She who works	Swedish
Imogene	Great mind	Latin
Irene	Goddess of peace	Greek
Iris	Flower	Greek
Irma	Noble guard	Teutonic
Isabel	Blessed	Spanish
Isadora	Gifted	Spanish
Isolde	Fair maiden	Irish
Jacqueline	Supplanter	French
Jamina	Dove	Arab
Jane, Joan, Janet		
	Grace of God	Hebrew
Jocelyn	Merry	Latin
Josephine	Increase	Hebrew
Judith	Praise of the Lord	Hebrew
June	Of Juno	Latin
Julia, Jewel	Curly haired	Latin
Katherine, Kay, Kitty		
	Purity	Latin
Letty	Joyful	Latin
Lala	Tulip	Slavic
Laura, Lorna	Laurel crowned	Roman
Libby	Shapely	Irish
Lillian	Flower	English
Linnea	Wild flower	Swedish
Louise, Lou, Lulu		
	Honored, brave	Teutonic
Lucy, Lucile	Born at daylight	Latin
Lydia	Woman of Lydia	Latin
Mabel, Maybelle	Jolly	French
Magdalene, Madeline		
	Favored	Hebrew
Margaret, Margot, Greta		
	Child of light	Italian
Martha	Lady	Hebrew
Mary, Marie, Marion		
	Star of the sea	Hebrew
Matilda, Maud	Heroine	Teutonic
May	Flourishing	Latin

Name	Meaning	Origin
Mercedes	Favored	Spanish
Mercy	Mercy	English
Michon	Goddess	French
Mignon	Pretty one	French
Mildred	Mild kind	Saxon
Millicent	Strength	Teutonic
Monica, Mona	Lovely	Greek
Muriel, Myrtle	Myrrh, an exotic woman	Greek
Nadine	Hope	French
Naomi	Pleasant	Hebrew
Nathalie	Christmas child	Latin
Nicolette, Colette	Victory	Norman
Nina, Ninon	Grace	Hebrew
Nona	Ninth	Latin
Norah	Decided	Gallic
Norma, Nydia	Maid of the sea	Norman
Olga	Holy	Russian
Olive	Peace, joy	Latin
Opal	Gem	Latin
Orriel, Orah	Divine power	Teutonic
Othilia, Odyl	Rich maid	Teutonic
Pamela	Sweetness	English
Pansy	Thought	English
Patience	Patient	American
Patricia	Noble	Latin
Pauline	Little one	Hebrew
Pearl	Child of light	English
Penelope	Weaver	Greek
Pepita	Addition	Hebrew
Phoebe, Phebe	Light of life	Greek
Phyllis	Leaf	Greek
Priscilla	Long life	Greek
Prudence	Wisdom	Latin
Queenie	Queen like	Gallic
Rachel	Little lamb	Hebrew
Ramona	Meaning unknown	Am. Indian
Rebecca	A troth	Hebrew
Regina	A queen	Latin
Renee	Re-born	French
Rhoda	Rose	Greek
Romola	Fame	Latin
Rosa, Rosalie	A rose	Latin

NAME	MEANING	ORIGIN
Ruby	A gem	English
Ruth	Contented	Hebrew
Sarah, Sallie, Sadie		
	Princess	Hebrew
Selma	Peaceful	Hebrew
Sibyl	Wise girl	Greek
Sigrid	Conqueror	Scand.
Signe	Blessing	Swedish
Solveig	Power of healing	Scand.
Sonia, Sonya, Sonja		
	Grand lady	Russian
Sophie	Wisdom	Greek
Stephany	Laurel crown	Greek
Suzanne, Susan	White lily	Greek
Sylvia	Wood-nymph	Greek
Thelma	Beloved maid	Teutonic
Theodora	Divine gift	Greek
Theresa	The reaper	Greek
Thora, Thyra	Goddess of thunder	Norse
Ulrica	Lady	Teutonic
Una	Born in famine	Celtic
Valerie	Skilled	Roman
Vera	Truth	Latin
Vega	Sea maid	Swedish
Verna, Laverne	Victory bringer	Greek
Vesta	Virgin	Roman
Victoria	Conqueror	Roman
Viola, Violet	Flower	Greek
Virginia	Flourishing	Latin
Vivian	Joy bringer	Roman
Wanda	Wanderer	Teutonic
Winifred, Wilma, Winnie		
	White browed	Keltic
Yolanda	Flower	Greek
Yvonne	Archer	French
Zara	Princess	Arab
Zenia, Zita	Hospitable	Russian
Zoe	Servant	French

Design
Danielle Marshall
and
Benjamin Darling

CPSIA information can be obtained at www.ICGtesting.com
Printed in the USA
BVOW07s2235280415

397957BV00002B/2/P